The Art of War by Sun Tzu

孙子兵法

SUN TZU (544 B.C. - 496 B.C.)

Translated and edited by
LINGKAI KONG

THE ART OF WAR

BY SUN TZU

This page intentionally left blank

Content

ACKNOWLEDGMENT

Lionel Giles's 1910 version gave the author of this translation a lot of inspiration, and the author was deeply impressed by the fruitful work of the predecessors.

The research project was funded by the Open Democracy and Science Foundation. The publication was supported by the Istanbul Institute of Political Strategy.

Thanks to Changling Kong and Gongdo Muhali for their review and comments on this book. Wenxian Lee also made constructive suggestions on the content of this book.

ABOUT THE TRANSLATOR

Lingkai Kong. PhD candidate in Political Science, Izmir University of Economics, Turkey. He received his bachelor degree in Economics from Beijing Foreign Studies University, China, and master degree in Economics from the University of Zurich, Switzerland. He is currently publishing a book titled: *The Philosophical Reviews of International Politics*. He is the manager of the *Journal of Politics and Strategy* and co-founder of the Open Democracy and Science Foundation.

His main areas of research include federalism, political philosophy, and democratic theory.

PREFACE

Sun Tzu (544 B.C.-496 B.C.) was a prominent military theorist and statesman in ancient China. During China's Spring and Autumn Period (a period of chaos and civil war), Sun Tzu served in the state of Wu, helping the monarch to revitalize the state and defeat its archrival Chu. He summarized his military career and wrote the book *Art of War*, which provided valuable research materials for future generations.

Unlike using Lionel Giles' 1910 translation directly, the author has retranslated and re-edited Sun Tzu's *Art of War* to make it more readable. Although Lionel Giles' translation is classic and outstanding, the translator of this book believes that due to its age and Lionel Giles' lack of understanding of some specific ancient Chinese language, some of the translation still could be improved. For example, the Chinese word "庙算" is directly translated by Lionel Giles as "calculation in the temple," but we translate it more accurately as "calculation and planning in the imperial court ". As a unit of distance, "Li" is directly translated as "Li" by Lionel Giles, which causes a lot of confusion to non-Chinese readers. In this version, we translate "Li" as "mile" to make it easier for readers to understand immediately. The translator feels this improved version of Sun Tzu's The Art of War is more fluid and intelligible due to significant revisions made to other sections.

We provide a version of the Chinese and English translations with cross-references for bilingual readers to compare and contrast, as well as for certain Chinese calligraphy fans to collect.

The entire *The Art of War*, if summed up in one sentence, is "the more wins the less, the strong wins the weak, and the superior wins the weak", and the rest of the contents can be regarded as the notes of this sentence. But how to judge the specific strength and weakness of the battlefield requires the general to make detailed judgments about the terrain, intelligence, the organization of his own army and of the opponent's army. Sun Tzu suggested "If you know the enemy and know yourself, you need not fear the result of a hundred battles. If you know yourself but not the enemy, for every victory gained you will also suffer a defeat. If you know neither the enemy nor yourself, you will succumb in every battle."

When the intelligence of the battlefield is mastered, and a strong force is used to combat a weak enemy, then victory is a natural thing. The result of victory in war is not known after the battle; it is already decided before the battle begins. That is : win the war before the battle begins.

Sun Tzu's military thinking is not only instructive for ancient generals, but also inspiring for today's readers, in international politics and even in business strategies. We hope that our publication of this edition will bring readers a good reading experience.

December 30, 2022
Istanbul

Lingkai Kong 孔凌恺

"If you know the enemy and know yourself, you need not fear the result of a hundred battles. If you know yourself but not the enemy, for every victory gained you will also suffer a defeat. If you know neither the enemy nor yourself, you will succumb in every battle."

-- Sun Tzu

1、始计篇 Laying Plans

I. Laying Plans
始计篇

Sun Tzu said: The art of war is crucial to the state. It is a matter of life and death, a choice between preservation and destruction. Consequently, it is an issue that cannot be ignored.

The art of war is therefore regulated by five constant characteristics that must be considered while attempting to identify the conditions on the battlefield. These include: (1) The moral law; (2) Heaven[1]; (3) Earth; (4) The commander; (5) The discipline. The moral law causes the people to be in total agreement with

---

[1] In traditional Chinese philosophy, Heaven and Earth are a collection of related ideas. Heaven can relate to the weather, the seasons, or the passage of time. The term Earth denotes specific geographical convenience.

their monarch, so that they will obey the monarch regardless of the risk to their lives. Heaven represents night and day, cold and heat, seasons and times. Earth is comprised of vast and minute distances, danger and safety, open land and narrow passes, and the possibilities of life and death. The commander represents the virtues of intelligence, sincerity, benevolence, courage and strictness. The discipline refers to the organization of the army into its correct sub-units, the ranking of officers, and the management of military expenditures. Every general should be familiar with these five rules. Whomever knows them will win; whoever does not will be defeated. Therefore, when attempting to determine the military conditions, you should base your reasoning on the following factors: Which of the two sovereigns possesses the moral law? Which of the two generals is more skilled? (3) Who holds the Heaven and Earth mandate? (4) On which side is discipline enforced most effectively? Which army is more more highly trained? (6) Which side has more well trained officers and soldier? (7) Which army has the most consistent system of rewards and punishments? Using these seven factors, I am able to predict victory or defeat.

The general who heeds my advice and implements it will succeed; let him stay in charge[2]. The general who does not heed my advice or act upon it will be defeated; he should be dismissed! While pursuing victory in accordance with my advice, advantageous circumstances will be employed to aid the battle conditions. Depending on the advantageous or unfavorable circumstances, one must

[2] Art of War by Sun Tzu was initially composed and delivered to the monarch. Therefore, this essay has the following recommendation: fire unqualified generals.

adjust their strategies.

All warfare is based on deception. Therefore, when we are able to attack, we must appear unable; when we are employing our troops, we must appear inactive; when we are close, we must convince the adversary that we are far away, and when we are far away, we must convince him that we are close. Use lures to tempt the adversary. Feign disarray, and crush him. If he is always prepared, defend against him. If he is stronger than you, avoid him. If his temperament is choleric, attempt to aggravate him. If he is cautious, make him arrogant by feigning weakness. If he is taking it easy, do not give him a break. If his forces are united, divide them. Attack him where he is unprepared; make your appearance where he is not anticipated. These military devices, which will lead to victory, must not be disclosed in advance.

The commander who wins a fight performs numerous calculations at his imperial court[3] before a battle is fought. The commander who loses a fight makes few pre-combat calculations. Thus, performing numerous computations leads to victory, while performing few calculations or none at all leads to defeat. At this moment, I can predict who will likely win or lose.

The original Chinese text

始计篇

孙子曰：兵者，国之大事，死生之地，

---

[3] The original Chinese text is "miao suan", which directly translates to "calculation at the temple", but the Chinese "miao tang 庙堂" actually means "imperial court" and not a real temple. So here the translator uses "imperial court".

存亡之道，不可不察也。

故经之以五事，校之以计，而索其情：一曰道，二曰天，三曰地，四曰将、五曰法。道者，令民与上同意也，故可以与之死，可以与之生，而不畏危。天者，阴阳，寒暑、时制也。地者，远近、险易、广狭、死生也。将者，智、信、仁、勇、严也。法者，曲制、官道、主用也。凡此五者，将莫不闻，知之者胜，不知者不胜。故校之以计，而索其情，曰：主孰有道？将孰有能？天地孰得？法令孰行？兵众孰强？士卒孰练？赏罚孰明？吾以此知胜负矣。

将听吾计，用之必胜，留之；将不听吾计，用之必败，去之。计利以听，乃为之势，以佐其外。势者，因利而制权也。

兵者，诡道也。故能而示之不能，用而示之不用，近而示之远，远而示之近；利而诱之，乱而取之，实而备之，强而避之，怒而挠之，卑而骄之，佚而劳之，亲而离之。攻其无备，出其不意。此兵家之胜，不可先传也。

夫未战而庙算胜者，得算多也；未战
而庙算不胜者，得算少也。多算胜，
少算不胜，而况于无算乎？吾以此观
之，胜负见矣。

2、作战篇 Waging War

II. Waging War
作战篇

Sun Tzu said: In the operations of war, where there are a thousand swift chariots, as many heavy chariots, and a hundred thousand mail-clad soldiers, with enough provisions to carry them a thousand miles[4], the expenditure at home and the front, including the entertainment of guests, the items such as glue and paint, and the spent on chariots and armor, will amount to one thousand ounces of silver per day. This is the cost of assembling a one hundred thousand-man army.

---

[4] The original Chinese text is "Li," which is an old Chinese distance measurement unit. 1 "Li" unit is about equivalent to 0.5 kilometers. Throughout different historical periods in ancient China, the "Li" distance has varied. Thousands of "Li" indicate a long distance rather than exact distance. Therefore, for the convenience of the reader, "Li" has been translated into "mile" throughout this text.

When engaging in actual combat, if victory takes a long time to arrive, men's weapons will get dull and their fervor will wane. You will deplete your resources if you lay siege to a fortress[5]. If the campaign is prolonged, the state's resources will not be sufficient to withstand the burden. When your weapons are dulled, your fervor is dampened, your strength is drained, and your treasure is depleted, other chieftains will emerge to exploit your predicament. Then no man, regardless of intelligence, will be able to avert the results. Thus, although we have heard of foolish haste in combat, protracted delays have never been linked with intelligence. There is no instance of a

---

[5] The original Chinese text is "city", but "city" itself in Chinese can refer to a living community formed around the market, or a fortress with a certain defensive function. According to the context, the translator translates the Chinese word "city" as "fortress".

nation profiting from protracted fighting. One who is intimately familiar with the miseries of war is the only one who can fully comprehend its advantageous conduct.

The shrewd soldier never raises a second levy nor loads his supply wagons more than twice. Bring war supplies from home, but forage on the enemy to ensure that the army has sufficient sustenance. The nation is fatigued because it must transport food to the soldiers. Feeding the soldiers at a distance impoverishes the populace. The closeness of an army leads prices to rise, and rising prices further deplete the people's resources. When their resources are depleted, the peasantry will be subject to enormous exactions. With this loss of substance and exhaustion of strength, the homes of the people will be stripped bare, and seven-tenths of their income will be lost, while the government will spend six-tenths of its total revenue on broken chariots, worn-out horses, breast-plates and helmets, bows and arrows, spears and shields, protective mantles, draught-oxen, and heavy wagons.

Therefore, a prudent general engages in enemy reconnaissance. One enemy cartload of provisions is comparable to twenty of one's own, and one enemy picul of provisions is equivalent to twenty of one's own.

Now, in order for our troops to kill the enemy, they must be enraged; so that they may benefit from conquering the enemy, they must receive their rewards. Therefore, in chariot combat, when 10 or more chariots have been captured, those who captured the first should be awarded. The enemy's banners should be replaced with our own, seized chariots should be mixed with ours and employed alongside them, and captured men should be treated warmly and maintained in our army. This is known as utilizing the defeated opponent to increase one's own power.

In battle, your primary objective should be victory, not protracted campaigns. Thus, it is clear that the head of an army is the decider of the nation's fate and the individual who determines whether the nation will live in peace or peril.

The original Chinese text

作战篇

孙子曰：凡用兵之法，驰车千驷，革车千乘，带甲十万，千里馈粮，则内外之费，宾客之用，胶漆之材，车甲之奉，日费千金，然后十万之师举矣。

其用战也胜，久则钝兵挫锐，攻城则

力屈，久暴师则国用不足。夫钝兵挫锐，屈力殚货，则诸侯乘其弊而起，虽有智者，不能善其后矣。故兵闻拙速，未睹巧之久也。夫兵久而国利者，未之有也。故不尽知用兵之害者，则不能尽知用兵之利也。

善用兵者，役不再籍，粮不三载；取用于国，因粮于敌，故军食可足也。国之贫于师者远输，远输则百姓贫。近于师者贵卖，贵卖则百姓财竭，财竭则急于丘役。力屈、财殚，中原内虚于家。百姓之费，十去其七；公家之费，破车罢马，甲胄矢弩。戟楯蔽橹，丘牛大车，十去其六。

故智将务食于敌。食敌一钟，当吾二十钟；芑秆一石，当吾二十石。

故杀敌者，怒也；取敌之利者，货也。故车战，得车十乘已上，赏其先得者，而更其旌旗，车杂而乘之，卒善而养之，是谓胜敌而益强。

故兵贵胜，不贵久。故知兵之将，生民之司命，国家安危之主也。

3、谋攻篇 Attack by Stratagem

III. Attack by Stratagem
谋攻篇

Sun Tzu said: In the practical art of war, it is ideal to seize the enemy's state whole and intact; it is less desirable to shatter and destroy it. Also, it is preferable to recapture a whole army than to destroy it, as well as an entire regiment, detachment, or company[6]. Therefore, it is not supreme excellence to fight and win every war; supreme excellence consists in breaking the enemy's resistance without fighting.

Thus, the finest form of generalship is to thwart the opponent's intentions; the second best is to prevent the enemy's forces from converging; the third best is to assault the opposing army in the field;

---

[6] Regiment, detachment, or company are all specific military establishments.

and the worst policy of all is to besiege walled fortress. The guideline is to avoid besieging walled cities wherever possible. The preparation of mantlets, movable shelters, and different combat equipment will require three full months, and the piling up of mounds over against the walls will take three months more. Unable to control his anger, the general will throw his soldiers into the assault like swarming ants, resulting in one-third of his men being killed while the fortress remains unconquered. Such are the devastating consequences of a siege.

Therefore, a shrewd commander subdues the enemy's army without any combat; he captures their fortress without laying siege to them; and he overthrows their states without extensive military operations. He will contest the supremacy of the empire with his armies intact; his success will be complete without a single casualty. This is the method of attacking by stratagem.

If our troops outnumber the enemy's by ten to one, we should surround him; if by five to one, we should assault him; and if by two to one, we should divide our army in half. If we are evenly matched, we propose fight; if we are somewhat outnumbered, we avoid the opponent; otherwise, we escape from him. Thus, even if a tiny army fights obstinately, it must ultimately be taken by the greater force.

Now the general is the state's bulwark; if the bulwark is perfect in all respects, the state will be strong; if it is deficient, the state will be weak.

There are three ways a leader might cause disaster for his army: (1) By ordering the troops to advance or retreat without knowing whether it is feasible. This is known as hobbling the army. (2) By attempting to control an army in the same manner that he governs a state while being unaware of the conditions that exist in an army. This produces restlessness among the soldiers. (3) By employing his army's commanders without distinction due to ignorance of the military principle of situational adaptability. This affects the soldiers' trust. When the army is restless and mistrustful, other feudal princes are certain to cause trouble. This is nothing more than introducing disorder into the troops and throwing the triumph away.

Therefore, we may deduce that there are five requisites for victory: (1) He who understands when to fight and when not to fight will prevail. (2) He who can effectively manage both superior and weaker troops will prevail. (3) He who can lead the entire army motivated by the same spirit will prevail. (4) He who can have prepared himself, awaits an unprepared opponent, will prevail. (5) He who possesses military might and is not hindered by the sovereign will prevail.

Hence the saying: "If you know the enemy and know yourself, you need not fear the result of a hundred battles. If you know yourself but not the enemy, for every victory gained you will also suffer a defeat. If you know neither the enemy nor yourself, you will succumb in every battle"[7].

The original Chinese text

谋攻篇

[7] Because this sentence is too classic and famous, this paper directly adopts Lionel Giles's translation in 1910 without making any deletion.

孙子曰：夫用兵之法，全国为上，破国次之，全军为上，破军次之；全旅为上，破旅次之；全卒为上，破卒次之；全伍为上，破伍次之。是故百战百胜，非善之善者也；不战而屈人之兵，善之善者也。

故上兵伐谋，其次伐交，其次伐兵，其下攻城。攻城之法为不得已。修橹轒辒，具器械，三月而后成，距堙，又三月而后已。将不胜其忿而蚁附之，杀士三分之一而城不拔者，此攻之灾也。

故善用兵者，屈人之兵而非战也，拔人之城而非攻也，毁人之国而非久也，必以全争于天下。故兵不顿而利可全，此谋攻之法也。

故用兵之法，十则围之，五则攻之，倍则分之，敌则能战之，少则能逃之，不若则能避之。故小敌之坚，大敌之擒也。

夫将者，国之辅也。辅周，则国必强；辅隙，则国必弱。

故君之所以患于军者三：不知军之不可以进而谓之进，不知军之不可以退而谓之退，是谓"縻军"；不知三军之事，而同三军之政者，则军士惑矣；不知三军之权，而同三军之任，则军士疑矣。三军既惑且疑，则诸侯之难至矣，是谓"乱军引胜"。

故知胜有五：知可以战与不可以战者胜，识众寡之用者胜，上下同欲者胜，以虞待不虞者胜，将能而君不御者胜。此五者，知胜之道也。

故曰：知彼知己者，百战不殆；不知彼而知己，一胜一负，不知彼，不知己，每战必殆。

4、军形篇 Tactical Dispositions

IV. Tactical Dispositions
军形篇

Sun Tzu said: Good commanders would place themselves beyond the prospect of defeat before waiting for a chance to vanquish the adversary. It is up to us to protect ourselves from defeat, but the chance to defeat the enemy is offered by the opponent himself. Thus, a skilled commander can protect himself from defeat, but cannot be guaranteed of defeating the opponent. Thus the famous saying: victory is calculated, not made.

Security against defeat requires defensive tactics, while the potential to defeat the opponent necessitates offensive tactics. The defensive strength is adequate, but the attacking strength is inadequate[8]. Whomever is proficient in defense hides in the deepest caves of the earth, while whoever is skillful in assault emerges from the highest peaks of heaven. Thus, on the one hand, we possess the capacity to defend ourselves, and on the other, we possess the capacity to achieve an offensive triumph.

It is not the pinnacle of perfection to perceive success only when it is within the comprehension of the general populace. Neither is it the pinnacle of greatness if you battle and conquer and receive plaudits from the entire empire. To move a single hair is not indicative of considerable strength; to view the sun and moon is not indicative of acute vision; and to hear the rumble of thunder is not indicative of a keen ear. A skillful strategist, according to the

---

[8] Some versions also write: The attacking strength is adequate, but the defensive strength is inadequate.

ancients, is one who not only wins, but does it with ease. His successes earn him neither a reputation for intelligence nor for bravery. Instead, he wins his battles by never committing errors. It is the absence of errors that ensures the certainty of success, as it entails defeating an already vanquished foe. Therefore, the skilled strategist places himself in a position where failure is impossible and does not miss the opportunity to beat the adversary. Thus, in war, the triumphant strategist seeks battle only after the victory has been gained, whereas the strategist destined for failure fights first and then seeks victory. The great leader cultivates the moral law and sticks to discipline rigorously; thus, he has the ability to govern success.

Regarding military strategy, we have, first, measurement; second, quantity estimation; third, calculation; fourth, balancing of chances; and fifth, victory. Earth gave birth to measurement; measurement to estimation of quantity; estimation of quantity to calculation; calculation to balancing of chances; and balancing of chances to victory. A victorious army weighs against a defeated army is comparable to a pound of weight versus a single grain. The momentum of a victorious force is comparable to the release of water into a chasm that is one thousand fathoms deep.

The original Chinese text

军形篇

孙子曰：昔之善战者，先为不可胜，以待敌之可胜。不可胜在己，可胜在敌。故善战者，能为不可胜，不能使敌之可胜。故曰：胜可知，而不可为。

不可胜者，守也；可胜者，攻也。守则有余，攻则不足。善守者，藏于九地之下，善攻者，动于九天之上，故能自保而全胜也。

见胜不过众人之所知，非善之善者也；战胜而天下曰善，非善之善者也。故举秋毫不为多力，见日月不为明目，闻雷霆不为聪耳。古之所谓善战者，胜于易胜者也。故善战者之胜也，无智名，无勇功。故其战胜不忒，不忒者，其所措必胜，胜已败者也。故善战者，立于不败之地，而不失敌之败也。是故胜兵先胜而后求战，败兵先战而后求胜。善用兵者，修道而保法，故能为胜败之政。

兵法：一曰度，二曰量，三曰数，四曰称，五曰胜。地生度，度生量，量生数，数生称，称生胜。故胜兵若以镒称铢，败兵若以铢称镒。胜者之战民也，若决积水于千仞之溪者，形也。

5、兵势篇 The momentum

V. The Momentum
兵势篇

Sun Tzu said: The idea of commanding a large army is identical to that of commanding a small force: it is simply a matter of dividing their numbers. Fighting with a huge army is identical to fighting with a small army; it is simply a matter of establishing signs and signals. To guarantee that your whole army can resist the full force of the enemy's onslaught and stay unshaken, you must employ both direct and indirect maneuvers. This is the consequence of weakness and strength: that the impact of your army on your opponent may be comparable to a grindstone striking an egg.

In every combat, direct tactics may be utilized to enter the fray, but indirect tactics are required to achieve victory. Effectively employed indirect tactics are as inexhaustible as Heaven and Earth, as endless as the flow of rivers and streams; like the sun and moon, they finish just to begin again; like the four seasons, they pass away only to return again. There are no more than five musical notes, but their combinations produce more tunes than could ever be heard. There are just five main colors (blue, yellow, red, white, and black), yet when combined, they yield more hues than can ever be seen. There are just five primary tastes (sour, acrid, salty, sweet, and bitter), but their combinations produce more flavors than can be tasted. In warfare, there are only two types of attacks: direct and indirect. However, the combination of these two forms an infinite number of moves. The direct and indirect lead to one another in succession. It is like going in a circle. Who can exhaust their combination's possibilities?

The approach of the army is comparable to the surge of a river that will even carry stones along its path. The decision-making capacity is comparable to a falcon's perfectly timed dive, which enables it to attack and kill its prey. Therefore, a skilled strategist will initiate quickly and make decisions swiftly. Momentum[9] may be compared to the bending of a crossbow; choice can be compared to the pulling of a trigger. In the midst of the upheaval and confusion of combat, there may appear to be disorder, but there is actually none; in the midst of disarray and anarchy, your array may be without head or tail, but it will be impervious to defeat.

[9] " 势 " in Chinese is also translated as "energy" in some versions. It means: a factor that can be accumulated and exploded in an instant to determine the outcome. Advantages of terrain, increased morale, and enhanced financial resources can all improve this " 势 ". The translator believes that the translation as "momentum" is more appropriate.

Faked chaos presupposes impeccable discipline, simulated fear presupposes bravery, and simulated frailty presupposes power. Hiding order behind a shroud of chaos is only a matter of subdivision; concealing boldness behind a display of fear requires a reserve of latent momentum; and disguising strength as weakness requires tactical dispositions.

Thus, one who is adept at keeping the opponent on the move maintains deceptive appearances based on which the adversary will behave. He sacrifices something in order for the opponent to seize it. By luring the opponents with baits, he keeps them on the move; finally, he ambushes them with a select force. The astute strategist considers the effect of united momentum and does not place excessive demands on individuals. Consequently, he is able to select the proper persons and harness combined momentum. When he employs combined momentum, his battling forces resemble logs or stones in motion. For it is the nature of a log or stone to stay still on level ground and to move when on a slope; if four-cornered, to stop, and if round-shaped, to roll downhill.

Thus, the momentum generated by a skilled strategist is comparable to that of a spherical stone rolling down a mountain from a height of thousands of feet. So much has been said about momentum.

The original Chinese text

兵势篇

孙子曰：凡治众如治寡，分数是也；斗众如斗寡，形名是也；三军之众，可使必受敌而无败者，奇正是也；兵之所加，如以碫投卵者，虚实是也。

凡战者，以正合，以奇胜。故善出奇者，无穷如天地，不竭如江海。终而复始，日月是也。死而更生，四时是也。声不过五，五声之变，不可胜听也；色不过五，五色之变，不可胜观也；味不过五，五味之变，不可胜尝也；战势不过奇正，奇正之变，不可胜穷也。奇正相生，如循环之无端，孰能穷之哉！

激水之疾，至于漂石者，势也；鸷鸟之疾，至于毁折者，节也。故善战者，其势险，其节短。势如扩弩，节如发机。纷纷纭纭，斗乱而不可乱；浑浑沌沌，形圆而不可败。乱生于治，怯生于勇，弱生于强。治乱，数也；勇怯，势也；强弱，形也。

故善动敌者，形之，敌必从之；予之，敌必取之。以利动之，以卒待之。故善战者，求之于势，不责于人故能择人而任势。任势者，其战人也，如转木石。木石之性，安则静，危则动，方则止，圆则行。

故善战人之势，如转圆石于千仞之山
者，势也。

6、虚实篇

Weak Points and Strong

VI. Weak Points and Strong
虚实篇[10]

Sun Tzu said: Whoever is first on the battlefield and awaits the enemy's arrival will be prepared for war; whoever is second on the battlefield and must rush to the fight will come fatigued. Therefore, the astute strategist impresses his will on the adversary, but does not accept the adversary's will. By withholding benefits, he can entice the adversary to approach voluntarily, or by causing damage, he can prevent the opponent from approaching. If the

---

[10] "虚"and"实" which translates directly as, "illusory and real," refer to weaknesses and strengths in the military. A good strategist figures out the weaknesses and strengths of his side and keeps them secret from the enemy. Even your own strong points should be pretended to be weak, so that your position is "illusory" in the eyes of the enemy.

enemy is at ease, he can bother them; if they are well-fed, he can starve them out; and if they are peacefully tented, he can compel them to move. Appear where the enemy must move quickly to protect; advance fast to unanticipated locations. If an army marches in a hostile-free region, it can cover a great distance without trouble.

You can ensure the success of your attacks if you solely target undefended locations. You may secure the safety of your defense by occupying only invulnerable spots. Therefore, that general is adept in attack if his opponent does not know what to defend, and adept in defense if his opponent does not know what to attack. Such a magnificent art of discretion and concealment! The art teaches us to become invisible and inaudible, allowing us to control the enemy's fate. You can advance and be completely unstoppable if you target the enemy's weak places; you may be safe from pursuit if your movements are faster than the enemy's. Even though the opponent is protected by a high rampart and a deep ditch, we may force him to engage in combat if we choose to do so. Simply assault another location that he will be compelled to defend. If we do not intend to engage in combat, we can prevent the adversary from confronting us by dividing the camping line. We need just provide him with something unusual and inexplicable.

By determining the enemy's dispositions while staying unseen, we are able to keep our troops concentrated while the enemy's are dispersed. We can build a single, unified force, but the adversary must fragment into smaller groups. Thus, a whole will be pitted against constituent pieces, which means that we will outnumber the opposition.

Moreover, if we are able to strike a weaker army with a stronger one, our adversaries would be in dire straits. The location where we want to battle must remain secret; otherwise, the adversary would have to prepare for prospective attacks at several sites, and his forces will be dispersed in numerous directions. The numbers we will confront at any given location will be proportionally small.

For if the opponent fortifies his van, he will weaken his rear; if he fortifies his rear, he will weaken his van; if he fortifies his left, he will weaken his right; if he fortifies his right, he will weaken his left. If he sent troops everywhere, he will be weakened everywhere. Our numerical vulnerability is from having to prepare for potential assaults, while our numerical strength results from requiring our opponent to do the same.

Knowing the location and timing of the upcoming combat allows us to concentrate from enormous distances in preparation to fight. But if neither time nor location is known, the left wing will be unable to support the right, the right will be unable to support the left, and neither the van nor the rear will be able to support each other. In addition, the farthest elements of the army are more than hundred miles apart, and even the closest are several miles!

Despite the fact that, according to my estimation, Yue[11] men outnumber ours, this will not benefit them in terms of victory. Therefore, I assert that success is attainable. Even if the opponent is numerically superior, we can prevent him from engaging in combat. Plan in

---

[11] The State of Yue (2032 B.C. - 222 B.C.) was a vassal state in southeastern China during the Xia, Shang, Western Zhou, Spring and Autumn, and Warring States periods in ancient China. The location is near currently Suzhou and Yangzhou, China.

order to uncover his strategies and the possibility of his accomplishment. Stimulate him and determine his activity or inactivity level. Force him to unveil himself in order to determine his weak places. Compare the opposing army to your own so that you may determine where your strength is great and where it is lacking. The ultimate level of tactical disposition is concealment; conceal your dispositions, and you will be secure from the prying eyes of the most cunning spies and the manipulations of the most intelligent minds. How victory may be achieved using the enemy's own methods is something the masses cannot fathom. No one can see the strategy from which triumph is derived, but everyone can see the tactics by which I conquer. Do not replicate the strategies that won you one triumph; instead, let the limitless diversity of conditions dictate your strategies.

Military strategies are analogous to the natural behavior of water, which naturally avoids heights and rushes downwards. Therefore, in warfare, one must avoid the powerful and attack the weak. The flow of water is determined by the character of the terrain it traverses; a soldier's triumph is determined by the nature of his opponent. Consequently, just as water does not maintain a steady form, there are no constant circumstances in battle. One who is able to adapt his tactics in proportion to his opponent and therefore achieve victory may be referred to as a god-born captain.

Therefore, the five elements[12] are not

---

[12] Refers to metal, wood, water, fire, earth. They are the five basic elements that Chinese classical philosophers explain to build the world. There is a relationship of mutual promotion and mutual restraint among these elements. Metal restrains wood, wood restrains earth, earth restrains water, water restrains fire, and fire restrains metal.

always equally prevalent, and the four seasons alternate in their predominance. There are both short and long days, and the moon has both waxing and declining phases.

The original Chinese text

虚实篇

孙子曰：凡先处战地而待敌者佚，后处战地而趋战者劳，故善战者，致人而不致于人。能使敌人自至者，利之也；能使敌人不得至者，害之也，故敌佚能劳之，饱能饥之，安能动之。出其所不趋，趋其所不意。行千里而不劳者，行于无人之地也。

攻而必取者，攻其所不守也；守而必固者，守其所不攻也。故善攻者，敌不知其所守；善守者，敌不知其所攻。微乎微乎，至于无形。神乎神乎，至于无声，故能为敌之司命。进而不可御者，冲其虚也；退而不可追者。速而不可及也。故我欲战，敌虽高垒深沟，不得不与我战者，攻其所必救也；我不欲战，画地而守之，敌不得与我战者，乖其所之也。

故形人而我无形，则我专而敌分。我专为一，敌分为十，是以十攻其一也，则我众而敌寡；能以众击寡者，则吾之所与战者，约矣。吾所与战之地不可知，不可知，则敌所备者多；敌所备者多，则吾所与战者，寡矣。

故备前则后寡，备后则前寡，备左则右寡，备右则左寡，无所不备，则无所不寡。寡者，备人者也；众者，使人备己者也。

故知战之地，知战之日，则可千里而会战。不知战地，不知战日，则左不能救右，右不能救左，前不能救后，后不能救前，而况远者数十里，近者数里乎？

以吾度之，越人之兵虽多，亦奚益于胜败哉？故曰：胜可为也。敌虽众，可使无斗。故策之而知得失之计，作之而知动静之理，形之而知死生之地，角之而知有余不足之处。故形兵之极，至于无形。无形，则深间不能窥，智者不能谋。因形而错胜于众，众不能知；人皆知我所以胜之形，而莫知吾所以制胜之形。故其战胜不复，而应形于无穷。

夫兵形象水，水之形，避高而趋下，兵之形，避实而击虚。水因地而制流，兵因敌而制胜。故兵无常势，水无常形，能因敌变化而取胜者，谓之神。

故五行无常胜，四时无常位，日有短长，月有死生。

7、军争篇 Maneuvering

VII. Maneuvering
军争篇

Sun Tzu said: In times of war, the general receives his orders from the sovereign. After amassing an army and concentrating his forces, he must mix and harmonize its many components before erecting a camp. After that comes tactical maneuvering, which is the most challenging aspect. The problem of tactical manoeuvre is in transforming deception into transparency and misfortune into advantage.

Thus, taking a lengthy and roundabout route, after luring the opponent out of the road, then beginning after him while yet managing to achieve the objective before him, demonstrates an understanding of the artifice of deviation. With an army, maneuvering is useful; with an undisciplined mob, it is most perilous. If you mobilize a fully-equipped army in an attempt to gain an edge, you will likely be too late. Having a mobile squad for this reason necessitates the sacrifice of its luggage and supplies. Thus, if you tell your troops to roll up their buff-coats and perform forced marches without stopping day or night, reaching double the customary distance in a single stretch, and marching a hundred miles to gain an edge, the enemy will capture the leaders of all three of your divisions[13]. On this strategy, only one-tenth of your army will reach its target, since the more powerful soldiers will lead the way while the more jaded ones will fall behind. If you march fifty

---

[13] During the Spring and Autumn Period of China, the princes' forces were separated into the upper army, the middle army, and the lower army, which were collectively referred to as the three divisions. Later, the "three divisions" became the synonym for the whole army.

miles to outmaneuver the enemy, you will lose the leader of your first division and only fifty percent of your army will reach the objective. When thirty miles are marched with the same aim, two-thirds of an army will arrive. Then, we may assume that an army without its baggage train is lost; without food, it is lost; and without supply depots, it is lost. We cannot form partnerships unless we understand the intentions of our neighbors. We are unfit to lead an army on the march if we are unfamiliar with the country's terrain, including its mountains and forests, cliffs and ravines, marshes and swamps. Unless we use local advisers, we will be incapable of capitalizing on natural advantages. Practice deception in battle, and you will prevail. The circumstances will determine whether you should concentrate or divide your forces. Let your rapidity resemble that of the wind, and your density that of the forest. Be like fire in marauding and robbing, and be as immovable as a mountain. Let your intentions be as opaque and impenetrable as the darkness, then fall like a lightning bolt when you move. When you plunder a region, divide the booty among your soldiers; when you conquer additional territory, split it into allotments for the advantage of the military. Think and ponder before taking action. Whoever has mastered the art of deception will prevail. This is the art of maneuvering.

The *Book of Army Management*[14] says: The spoken word does not carry far enough on the battlefield; hence, gongs and drums are utilized. Also, ordinary things cannot be seen clearly enough, thus banners and flags must be utilized. Using gongs and drums, banners and

---

[14] A military book written in the preliminary formation stage of ancient Chinese military thought. It was probably written during the Western Zhou Dynasty.

flags, the army's ears and eyes may be directed to a certain location. As a result of the army creating a single, unified body, it is difficult for the courageous to advance or withdraw alone. This is the skill of interacting with huge groups of men. Make extensive use of signal fires and drums during night combat, and flags and banners during day combat, to attract the ears and eyes of your army.

An entire army can lose its spirit, and a commander-in-chief can lose his presence of mind. Now, a soldier's morale is at its peak in the morning, begins to wane about midday, and has only thoughts of returning to camp in the evening. A shrewd commander avoids an army while its morale is high, but assaults it when it is fatigued and eager to retreat. This is the art of emotions. Disciplined and composed, awaiting the arrival of chaos and confusion among the enemy, it is the art of maintaining composure. To be close to the objective while the opponent is still far away, to be at ease while the opponent labors and struggles, and to be well-fed while the opponent is hungry: this is the art of regulating one's power. To avoid encountering an opponent whose flags are in perfect order and to avoid assaulting an army arrayed calmly and confidently, it is the art of studying circumstance.

It is military doctrine not to advance uphill against the enemy nor to oppose him when he comes downhill; do not pursue an enemy who simulates flight; do not attack soldiers whose temper is strong; do not swallow bait offered by the enemy; do not interfere with an army returning home; leave an outlet open when surrounding an army; do not press a desperate foe too hard. This describes the art of war.

The original Chinese text

军争篇

孙子曰：凡用兵之法，将受命于君，合军聚众，交和而舍，莫难于军争。军争之难者，以迂为直，以患为利。

故迂其途，而诱之以利，后人发，先人至，此知迂直之计者也。军争为利，军争为危。举军而争利则不及，委军而争利则辎重捐。是故卷甲而趋，日夜不处，倍道兼行，百里而争利，则擒三将军，劲者先，疲者后，其法十一而至；五十里而争利，则蹶上将军，其法半至；三十里而争利，则三分之二至。是故军无辎重则亡，无粮食则亡，无委积则亡。故不知诸侯之谋者，不能豫交；不知山林、险阻、沮泽之形者，不能行军；不用乡导者，不能得地利。故兵以诈立，以利动，以分和为变者也。故其疾如风，其徐如林，侵掠如火，不动如山，难知如阴，动如雷震。掠乡分众，廓地分利，悬权而动。先知迂直之计者胜，此军争之法也。

《军政》曰："言不相闻，故为之金鼓；视不相见，故为之旌旗。"夫金鼓旌旗者，所以一民之耳目也。民既专一，则勇者不得独进，怯者不得独退，此用众之法也。故夜战多金鼓，昼战多旌旗，所以变人之耳目也。

三军可夺气，将军可夺心。是故朝气锐，昼气惰，暮气归。善用兵者，避其锐气，击其惰归，此治气者也。以治待乱，以静待哗，此治心者也。以近待远，以佚待劳，以饱待饥，此治力者也。无邀正正之旗，勿击堂堂之阵，此治变者也。

故用兵之法，高陵勿向，背丘勿逆，佯北勿从，锐卒勿攻，饵兵勿食，归师勿遏，围师遗阙，穷寇勿迫，此用兵之法也。

8、九变篇 Variation in Tactics

VIII. Variation in Tactics
九变篇

Sun Tzu said: In times of war, the general gets orders from the sovereign, gathers his army, and focuses his troops. In tough terrain, do not encamp. In terrain with intersecting roads, hold hands with your buddies. In dangerously remote terrains, do not remain. In confined circumstances, turn to subterfuge. In a dire situation, fight. There are roads that must not be taken, armies that must not be assaulted, fortresses that must not be besieged, positions that must not be fought, and sovereign orders that must not be carried out.

The general who fully comprehends the benefits of varying strategies is able to effectively command his men. The general who does not comprehend them may be familiar with the country's topography, but he will be unable to put his knowledge to practical use. Even if he is familiar with the five advantages, a student of war who is unfamiliar with the art of war of diversifying his plans will fail to make the best use of his forces.

Therefore, in the plans of a good leader, both advantages and disadvantages will be taken into account. If we limit our expectation of benefit in this manner, we may be able to carry out the core of our plans. If, on the other hand, in the middle of problems we are constantly ready to take an advantage, we may extract ourselves from catastrophe. Reduce the hostile leaders by inflicting injury on them; keep them continually occupied; hold out deceptive allurements, and make them rush to any given spot. The art of war teaches us to rely not on the possibility that the enemy will not arrive, but on our own preparation to receive him; not on the possibility that he will not assault, but on the fact that we have made our position impregnable.

There are five potentially fatal flaws that might afflict a general: (1) Recklessness, which leads to destruction; (2) cowardice, which leads to capture; (3) a hasty temper, which may be aroused by insults; (4) a delicacy of honor that is sensitive to disgrace; and (5) over-solicitude for his soldiers, which leaves him vulnerable to anxiety and difficulty. These are the five fatal faults of a general that are destructive to the conduct of war. When an army is defeated and its leader is killed, one of these five fatal flaws will undoubtedly be to blame. These cannot be disregarded.

九变篇

孙子曰：凡用兵之法，将受命于君，合军聚众。圮地无舍，衢地交合，绝地无留，围地则谋，死地则战，途有所不由，军有所不击，城有所不攻，地有所不争，君命有所不受。

故将通于九变之利者，知用兵矣；将不通九变之利，虽知地形，不能得地之利矣；治兵不知九变之术，虽知五利，不能得人之用矣。

是故智者之虑，必杂于利害，杂于利而务可信也，杂于害而患可解也。是故屈诸侯者以害，役诸侯者以业，趋诸侯者以利。故用兵之法，无恃其不来，恃吾有以待之；无恃其不攻，恃吾有所不可攻也。

故将有五危，必死可杀，必生可虏，忿速可侮，廉洁可辱，爱民可烦。凡

此五者，将之过也，用兵之灾也。覆
军杀将，必以五危，不可不察也。

9、行军篇

The Army on the March

IX. The Army on the March
行军篇

Sun Tzu said: Concerning the topic of army encampment and the observation of hostile signs: Pass swiftly across mountains, establishing positions based on the valley terrain. Do not climb heights to engage in combat. So much for mountain warfare. Once you have crossed a river, you should move away from it. Do not advance to meet an invading force in mid-stream when it crosses a river on its forward march. It is advisable to allow half the force to cross before launching an assault. If you are eager for battle, you should avoid meeting the invader near a river he must cross. Do not proceed upstream to meet the enemy; instead, moor your craft higher than the adversary. So much for river warfare. Your only concern when traversing salt marshes should be to do so fast and without delay. If you are compelled to battle on a salt-marsh, you should have grass and water close by, and your back should be against a group of trees. So much for salt-march operations. In flat, dry terrain, assume a readily accessible position with rising land to your right and behind you, so that the danger is in front of you and safety is behind you. So much for campaigning in flat terrains. These are the four disciplines of military expertise that allowed the Yellow Emperor[15] to defeat four distinct sovereigns.

All armies like high terrain over low and sunny locations over gloomy ones. If you take care of your troops and camp

---

[15] Yellow Emperor (2717 B.C? - 2599 B.C.?), a figure in ancient legends. He is the leader of the tribal alliance in ancient China, and he is honored as the "humanistic ancestor" of China and the blood relative ancestor of the Chinese nation.

on hard ground, the army will be free of any type of sickness, ensuring victory. When approaching a hill, take the sunny side with the slope on your right. Thus, you will simultaneously operate for the benefit of your warriors and take use of the terrain's inherent advantages.

When a river you desire to ford is swollen and foamy due to severe rainfall, you must wait until it stabilizes before crossing.

The terrain with steep cliffs with streams flowing between them, deep natural hollows, limited areas, dense thickets, quagmires, and crevasses should be abandoned as quickly as possible and not approached. While we avoid such locations, we should entice the enemy to approach them; while we confront them, we should provide them to the adversary's rear.

In the vicinity of your camp, any steep terrain, ponds surrounded by aquatic vegetation, deep basins filled with reeds, or woodlands with heavy undergrowth must be thoroughly routed out and investigated, as these are possible hiding spots for ambush hunters and cunning spies.

When the enemy is close and silent, he relies on the inherent power of his position. When he maintains his distance and attempts to instigate a fight, he is eager for the opposing side to advance. If his campsite is easily accessible, he is offering a bait.

Motion amid the forest's trees indicates that the adversary is advancing. The emergence of a lot of blocks amidst dense vegetation indicates that the enemy is attempting to arouse our suspicions. The rise of birds is an indication of an ambush. Creatures that are alarmed suggest that a surprise onslaught is imminent. When dust rises in a tall column, it indicates the arrival of chariots; when the dust is low and widespread, it indicates the approach of soldiers. It indicates that opponents have been despatched to collect firewood when it branches off in several directions. A few moving dust clouds indicate that the army is setting up camp.

Words of humility and greater preparations are indicators that the enemy is preparing to advance. The use of violent words and advancing as if to assault are indicators that he will retreat. When the light chariots emerge first and arrange themselves on the wings, it indicates that the adversary is preparing for combat. Peace offers without a sworn covenant are indicative of a scheme. When many soldiers are fleeing, it indicates that the decisive time has arrived. When some are seen approaching and others receding, this serves as an enticement.

When the soldiers rely on their spears for support, they are weak from hunger. If those who are dispatched to collect water begin to drink themselves, the army is parched. If the opponent recognizes a potential advantage but makes no attempt to achieve it, the men will be weary. If birds congregate at a location, it is vacant. Nighttime commotion indicates anxiousness. If there is unrest in the camp, the authority of the commander is weakened. If banners and flags are being moved around, sedition is in the works. Officers' anger indicates that the soldiers are exhausted. When an army feeds its horses with grain and slaughters its cattle for sustenance, and when the men do not hang their cooking pots over the campfires as a sign that they will not return to their tents, you may assume that they want to fight to the death. The sight of men chatting in hushed tones or muttering in small groups indicates discontent among the rank and file. Too many awards indicate that the opponent has exhausted his resources, while too many punishments indicate that he is in grave straits. To begin with bravado and then succumb to fear due to the enemy's numbers demonstrates an extreme lack of intellect. When an adversary sends envoys with praises in their tongues, it indicates a desire for a cease-fire. If the enemy's forces advance enraged and remain confronting ours for an extended period of time without engaging in combat or withdrawing, extreme alert and caution are required.

If our forces are the same size as the enemy's, it is more than insufficient; it just means that no direct attack can be launched. Simply focus all of our available resources, keep a tight eye on the adversary, and call for reinforcements. Whoever lacks preparation and derides his opponents is certain to be caught by them.

If troops are disciplined prior to developing an attachment to you, they will not be subservient, and if they are not submissive, they will be essentially worthless. If sanctions are not implemented while the troops have been devoted to you, they will continue to be unless. Therefore, troops must be handled with kindness in the first instance, but kept under control with iron discipline. This is a certain path to triumph. If directives are consistently implemented during training, the army will be well-disciplined; otherwise, its discipline would be poor. If a general has faith in his troops yet consistently insists on their obedience, both he and his troops will benefit.

The original Chinese text

行军篇

孙子曰：凡处军相敌：绝山依谷，视生处高，战隆无登，此处山之军也。绝水必远水；客绝水而来，勿迎之于水内，令半济而击之，利；欲战者，无附于水而迎客；视生处高，无迎水流，此处水上之军也。绝斥泽，惟亟去无留；若交军于斥泽之中，必依水草而背众树，此处斥泽之军也。平陆处易，而右背高，前死后生，此处平陆之军也。凡此四军之利，黄帝之所以胜四帝也。

凡军好高而恶下，贵阳而贱阴，养生而处实，军无百疾，是谓必胜。丘陵堤防，必处其阳，而右背之。此兵之利，地之助也。

上雨，水沫至，欲涉者，待其定也。

凡地有绝涧、天井、天牢、天罗、天陷、天隙，必亟去之，勿近也。吾远之，敌近之；吾迎之，敌背之。

军行有险阻、潢井、葭苇、山林、蘙荟者，必谨覆索之，此伏奸之所处也。

敌近而静者，恃其险也；远而挑战者，欲人之进也；其所居易者，利也。

众树动者，来也；众草多障者，疑也；鸟起者，伏也；兽骇者，覆也；尘高而锐者，车来也；卑而广者，徒来也；散而条达者，樵采也；少而往来者，营军也。

辞卑而益备者，进也；辞强而进驱者，退也；轻车先出居其侧者，陈也；无约而请和者，谋也；奔走而陈兵车者，期也；半进半退者，诱也。

杖而立者，饥也；汲而先饮者，渴也；见利而不进者，劳也；鸟集者，虚也；夜呼者，恐也；军扰者，将不重也；旌旗动者，乱也；吏怒者，倦也；粟马肉食，军无悬瓺，不返其舍者，穷寇也；谆谆翕翕，徐与人言者，失众也；数赏者，窘也；数罚者，困也；
先暴而后畏其众者，不精之至也；来
委谢者，欲休息也。兵怒而相迎，久
而不合，又不相去，必谨察之。

兵非益多也，惟无武进，足以并力、
料敌、取人而已。夫惟无虑而易敌者，
必擒于人。

卒未亲附而罚之，则不服，不服则难
用也。卒已亲附而罚不行，则不可用
也。故令之以文，齐之以武，是谓必
取。令素行以教其民，则民服；令不
素行以教其民，则民不服。令素行者，
与众相得也。

10、地形篇 Terrain

X. Terrain
地形篇

Sun Tzu said: There are six distinct types of terrain: (1) Accessible ground; (2) entangling ground; (3) temporizing ground; (4) narrow passes; (5) precipitous heights; and (6) enemy positions at a long distance. Ground that may be traveled freely by both sides is referred to as accessible. Regarding this type of terrain, seize the elevated and sunny places before the enemy and carefully secure your supply line. Then you will have an advantage in battle. Entangling describes land that may be abandoned but is difficult to reoccupy. From such a position, if the adversary is unprepared, you can advance and beat him. However, if the opponent is prepared for your arrival and you fail to beat him, it will be hard to return, and calamity will result. Temporizing ground refers to a position in which neither side will gain by making the first move. In this situation, even if the opponent offers us an alluring bait, it is prudent not to advance, but rather to retreat, thereby luring the enemy in his turn; then, when a portion of his army has emerged, we may launch our attack with advantage. Regarding narrow passes, if you can seize them early, garrison them heavily and await the arrival of the enemy. Should the army prevent you from occupying a pass, pursue him only if the pass is little garrisoned and not if it is heavily garrisoned. If you are in advance of your opponent on precipitous heights, you should occupy the elevated and sunny locations and wait for him to ascend. If the opponent has already conquered the territory, withdraw and attempt to lure him away. If you are located at a great distance from the adversary and both armies are of comparable power, it is difficult to initiate a combat, and fighting will be to your detriment. These six are the Earth's fundamental principles. The general who has acquired a position of authority must study them thoroughly.

Now an army is subject to six distinct tragedies, none of which result from natural causes but rather from the general's errors. These are: (1) Flight, (2) insubordination, (3) collapse, (4) ruin, (5) disorganization, and (6) rout. Other variables being equal, if one force is thrown against another force that is 10 times its magnitude, the outcome will be flight. When the troops are too powerful and their superiors are too weak, insubordination occurs. When the officers are too powerful and the soldiers are too weak, collapse ensues. Before the commander-in-chief can determine whether or not he is able to fight, when the superior officers are enraged and disobedient and, upon encountering the enemy, give battle on their own account out of resentment, the outcome is ruin. When the general is weak and without authority; when his commands are not clear and explicit; when there are no fixed responsibilities given to officers and soldiers; and when the ranks are organized in a slovenly and disorderly way, the outcome is complete disorganization. When a general, unable to predict the enemy's strength, permits an inferior force to fight a greater force, or sends a weak detachment against a strong army, and fails to position elite soldiers in the front ranks, rout is certain. The general who has acquired a position of responsibility must pay close attention to these six ways of inviting loss.

The terrain is the soldier's greatest ally, but the test of a great general is the ability to estimate the enemy, command the forces of victory, and calculate problems, risks, and distances with shrewdness. He will win his conflicts if he understands these concepts and applies them in combat. Whoever neither knows nor follows them will undoubtedly be vanquished.

If fighting will certainly end in victory, you must fight even if the ruler forbids it; if fighting will not result in victory, you must not fight even if the ruler orders you to. State's crown gem is the general who advances without desiring renown and returns without fearing humiliation, whose only aim is to defend his nation and serve his monarch well.

Consider your soldiers as your children, and they will follow you into the most treacherous valleys; consider them as your own cherished sons, and they will remain with you till the end. If, however, you are lenient but unable to assert your authority, compassionate but unable of enforcing your orders, and incapable of restraining chaos, then your soldiers must be compared to spoiled children and they serve no practical function.

If we know that our own troops are ready to strike, but are ignorant that the enemy is not, we are just halfway to achieving victory. If we know that the adversary is vulnerable to assault but are ignorant that our own troops are unable to attack, we are only halfway to achieving victory. If we know that the opponent is vulnerable to assault and that our soldiers are prepared to strike, but are uninformed that the terrain makes battle impractical, we are only halfway to achieving victory. Therefore, once in motion, an experienced leader is never confused; once he has left camp, he is never at a loss. Thus the proverb: If you know the enemy and you know yourself, your triumph is assured; if you know Heaven and you know Earth, you may complete your victory.

The original Chinese text

地形篇

孙子曰：地形有通者，有挂者，有支者，有隘者，有险者，有远者。我可以往，彼可以来，曰通；通形者，先居高阳，利粮道，以战则利。可以往，难以返，曰挂；挂形者，敌无备，出而胜之；敌若有备，出而不胜，难以返，不利。我出而不利，彼出而不利，曰支；支形者，敌虽利我，我无出也；引而去之，令敌半出而击之，利。隘形者，我先居之，必盈之以待敌；若敌先居之，盈而勿从，不盈而从之。险形者，我先居之，必居高阳以待敌；若敌先居之，引而去之，勿从也。远形者，势均，难以挑战，战而不利。
凡此六者，地之道也；将之至任，不

可不察也。

故兵有走者，有弛者，有陷者，有崩者，有乱者，有北者。凡此六者，非天之灾，将之过也。夫势均，以一击十，曰走；卒强吏弱，曰弛，吏强卒弱，曰陷；大吏怒而不服，遇敌怼而自战，将不知其能，曰崩；将弱不严，教道不明，吏卒无常，陈兵纵横，曰乱；将不能料敌，以少合众，以弱击强，兵无选锋，曰北。凡此六者，败之道也；将之至任，不可不察也。

夫地形者，兵之助也。料敌制胜，计险厄远近，上将之道也。知此而用战者必胜，不知此而用战者必败。

故战道必胜，主曰无战，必战可也；战道不胜，主曰必战，无战可也。故进不求名，退不避罪，唯人是保，而利合于主，国之宝也。

视卒如婴儿，故可与之赴深溪；视卒如爱子，故可与之俱死。厚而不能使，爱而不能令，乱而不能治，譬若骄子，不可用也。

知吾卒之可以击，而不知敌之不可击，胜之半也；知敌之可击，而不知吾卒之不可以击，胜之半也；知敌之可击，知吾卒之可以击，而不知地形之不可以战，胜之半也。故知兵者，动而不迷，举而不穷。故曰：知彼知己，胜乃不殆；知天知地，胜乃不穷。

11、九地篇

The Nine Situations

XI. The Nine Situations
九地篇

Sun Tzu said: The art of war identifies nine types of ground[16]: (1) dispersive ground, (2) facile ground, (3) contentious ground, (4) open ground, (5) ground of intersecting roads, (6) serious ground, (7) difficult ground, (8) hemmed-in ground, and (9) desperate ground. When a chieftain fights within his own territory, the terrain is dispersive. When he has advanced a small distance into hostile territory, it is considered facile ground. Contentious ground is land whose holding confers substantial benefits to both parties. Open ground is land on which both sides have freedom of movement. roads

---

[16] Sometimes translated as "situation", "terrain" or "country". They both refer to the place where the war take place.

intersect on land that is the key to three contiguous states, such that whomever occupies it first controls the majority of the empire. When an army penetrates the heart of an enemy nation and leaves behind a number of walled cities, the situation is serious. Mountain forests, rugged steeps, marshes and fens—all country that is hard to traverse: this is difficult ground.   This is hemmed-in territory, which can only be accessed by tiny gorges and from which we can only retreat via convoluted pathways, so that a small number of the enemy is sufficient to crush a huge number of our men. Ground that can only be spared from destruction via immediate combat is desperate ground. On dispersive ground, there should be no fighting. On facile ground, one should not stop. On contentious ground, do not attack. On open ground, do not attempt to obstruct the enemy's path. On the ground at highway intersections, hold hands with your buddies. On serious terrain, amass plunder. In difficult terrain, maintain a steady march. On a hemmed-in ground, resort to subterfuge. On desperate ground, fight.

Those who were considered skilled commanders in the past understood how to dig a hole between the enemy's front and rear; to prevent cooperation between his large and small divisions; to prevent good troops from rescuing poor troops and superiors from rallying men. When the enemy's forces were unified, they were able to throw them into chaos. When it was advantageous for them to advance, they did so; otherwise, they stood motionless. If asked how to deal with a large enemy force arrayed and on the verge of launching an attack, I would reply, "Start by capturing something that your opponent holds dear; then he will submit to your will."

The essence of battle is swiftness: take advantage of the enemy's unreadiness, go through unanticipated paths, and strike undefended positions.

The following are the guiding principles for an invading force: The further you penetrate a country, the greater the cohesion of your forces, and thus the defenders will be unable to defeat you. Make incursions into rich areas to provide food for your troops. Examine the well-being of your troops with care, and do not overwork them. Concentrate your strength and reserve your energy. Keep your army in constant motion and invent ingenious strategies. Place your men in locations from where there is no escape, and they will choose death over escape. If they are willing to confront death, they can do anything. Officers and men alike will exert their greatest effort. In desperate situations, soldiers lose their fear. If there is no sanctuary, they will remain steadfast. If they are in an enemy nation, they will present a resolute front. If no assistance is available, they will fight fiercely. Thus, without waiting to be marshaled, the troops will be continually on the alert; without waiting to be requested, they will fulfill your will; without restrictions, they will be loyal; and without orders, they may be relied upon. Prohibit the use of omens and eliminate superstitious concerns. Then, until death itself, there is nothing to dread. If our soldiers are not overwhelmed with wealth, it is not because they dislike wealth, and if their lifespans are not too lengthy, it is not because they dislike living long lives. Your troops may grieve on the day they are ordered into war, with those seated bedewing their clothing and those supine allowing tears to trickle down their cheeks. But once they are subdued, they will demonstrate the valor of a Zhu or a Gui[17].

The skilled strategist is comparable to Shuai Ran[18]. Now, the Shuai Ran is a snake that lives in the Chang Mountains. If you strike its head, you will be attacked by its tail; if you strike its tail, you will be attacked by its head; and if you strike its middle, you will be attacked by both its head and tail.

If asked if an army can be built to resemble the Shuai Ran, I would respond affirmatively. For while the men of Wu and the men of Yue are adversaries, if they are trapped in a storm while crossing a river in the same boat, they will aid each other like the left hand assists the right. Therefore, relying

---

[17] Zhu and Gui. Famous military leaders during the Spring and Autumn and Warring States Periods of China.
[18] Shuai Ran. A legendary snake from classical Chinese mythology. Often used in ancient Chinese military science as a metaphor in formations.

solely on the tying of horses and the burial of chariot wheels is insufficient. The premise for managing an army is to establish a single standard of bravery that everyone must meet. How to make the most of both strong and weak is a question pertaining to ground usage. In this manner, the shrewd general leads his army as if he were leading a single soldier by the hand.

A general's duty is to be reticent and therefore maintain secret; honest and just and thus maintain order. He must be able to mislead his officers and soldiers with phony reports and appearances, keeping them completely in the dark. By shifting his arrangements and strategies, he prevents the opposition from gaining definitive information. By relocating his camp and taking convoluted paths, he keeps the adversary from predicting his objective. At the decisive time, an army's leader acts as though he has ascended a height and then kicked away the ladder behind him. He leads his forces far into dangerous area before revealing his intentions. He destroys his vessels and shatters his cooking pots; like a shepherd leading a flock of sheep, he pushes his soldiers in all directions, and no one knows where he is headed. To assemble his troops and lead them into danger: this is the general's responsibility. The many measures appropriate to the nine types of terrain, the efficacy of offensive or defensive strategies, and the underlying laws of human nature must all be thoroughly investigated.

When entering enemy territory, the general rule is that deep penetration leads to cohesiveness, whilst shallow penetration results in dispersion. When you leave your home nation and take your troops into neighboring territory, you find yourself in a precarious position. When there are means of connection on all four sides, the terrain consists of roads that intersect. When one penetrates far into a country, one is on serious territory. When you penetrate only a little distance, the ground is facile. It is hemmed-in ground when enemy strongholds are in your rear and there are narrow paths in front of you. When there is no refuge whatsoever, the ground is desperate.

Therefore, on dispersive ground, I would inspire my men with unity of purpose. On facile ground, I would see that there is close connection between all parts of my army. On contentious ground, I would hurry up my rear. On open ground, I would keep a vigilant eye on my defenses. On ground of intersecting roads, I would consolidate my alliances. On serious ground, I would try to ensure a continuous stream of supplies. On difficult ground, I would keep pushing on along the road. On hemmed-in ground, I would block any way of retreat. On desperate ground, I would proclaim to my soldiers the hopelessness of saving their lives.

For it is in the nature of the soldier to provide tenacious opposition when encircled, to fight fiercely when helpless, and to yield quickly when in peril. We cannot form an alliance with neighboring rulers unless we understand their intentions. We are unfit to lead an army on the march if we are unfamiliar with the country's terrain, including its mountains and forests, cliffs and ravines, marshes and swamps. If we do not use local advisors, we will be incapable of capitalizing on natural advantages. A ruler who disregards any of the following four or five principles is unfit for battle. When a warlike monarch assaults a great state, his generalship is demonstrated by keeping the enemy's armies from congregating. He intimidates his adversaries, preventing their friends from uniting against him. Consequently, he does not attempt to form alliances with everyone, nor does he promote the power of other nations. He executes his own hidden plans, leaving his adversaries in amazement. Thus, he is in a position to take their cities and overturn their kingdoms. You will be able to command an entire army as if you were dealing with a single soldier if you grant prizes without respect for the rules and give instructions without consideration for prior agreements. Confront your men with the act itself; never reveal your plan to them. When the prognosis is favorable, convey it to them, but remain silent when the situation is bleak.

Place your army in mortal danger, and it will survive; place it in dire difficulties, and it will emerge intact. For it is only when a power has been exposed to danger that it might strike a decisive victory.

To achieve success in battle, we must carefully adapt to the enemy's objectives. By relentlessly clinging to the enemy's flank, we will eventually kill the enemy's commander-in-chief. This is referred to as the capacity to accomplish anything by cunning.

On the day you assume charge, block the boundary passages, erase the official tally, and prevent all emissaries from passing. Be firm in the council chamber in order to maintain control of the situation. If the opponent leaves an open entrance, you must enter immediately. Defeat your opponent by grabbing what he values most, and gently timing his descent to the earth. Follow the prescribed course and adapt to the adversary until you can engage in decisive combat. First, display the coyness of a maiden until the opponent provides you an opportunity; then, imitate the speed of a running hare, and the enemy will be unable to resist you.

The original Chinese text

九地篇

孙子曰：用兵之法，有散地，有轻地，有争地，有交地，有衢地，有重地，有圮地，有围地，有死地。诸侯自战其地，为散地。入人之地不深者，为轻地。我得则利，彼得亦利者，为争地。我可以往，彼可以来者，为交地。诸侯之地三属，先至而得天下之众者，为衢地。入人之地深，背城邑多者，为重地。行山林、险阻、沮泽，凡难行之道者，为圮地。所由入者隘，所从归者迂，彼寡可以击吾之众者，为围地。疾战则存，不疾战则亡者，为死地。是故散地则无战，轻地则无止，

争地则无攻，交地则无绝，衢地则合
交，重地则掠，圮地则行，围地则谋，
死地则战。

所谓古之善用兵者，能使敌人前后不
相及，众寡不相恃，贵贱不相救，上
下不相收，卒离而不集，兵合而不齐。
合于利而动，不合于利而止。敢问：
"敌众整而将来，待之若何？"曰：
"先夺其所爱，则听矣。"

兵之情主速，乘人之不及，由不虞之
道，攻其所不戒也。

凡为客之道：深入则专，主人不克；
掠于饶野，三军足食；谨养而勿劳，
并气积力，运兵计谋，为不可测。投
之无所往，死且不北，死焉不得，士
人尽力。兵士甚陷则不惧，无所往则
固。深入则拘，不得已则斗。是故其
兵不修而戒，不求而得，不约而亲，
不令而信，禁祥去疑，至死无所之。
吾士无余财，非恶货也；无余命，非
恶寿也。令发之日，士卒坐者涕沾襟。
偃卧者涕交颐。投之无所往者，诸、
刿之勇也。

故善用兵者，譬如率然；率然者，常山之蛇也。击其首则尾至，击其尾则首至，击其中则首尾俱至。敢问："兵可使如率然乎？"曰："可。"夫吴人与越人相恶也，当其同舟而济，遇风，其相救也如左右手。是故方马埋轮，未足恃也；齐勇若一，政之道也；刚柔皆得，地之理也。故善用兵者，携手若使一人，不得已也。

将军之事：静以幽，正以治。能愚士卒之耳目，使之无知。易其事，革其谋，使人无识；易其居，迂其途，使人不得虑。帅与之期，如登高而去其梯；帅与之深入诸侯之地，而发其机，焚舟破釜，若驱群羊，驱而往，驱而来，莫知所之。聚三军之众，投之于险，此谓将军之事也。九地之变，屈伸之利，人情之理，不可不察。

凡为客之道：深则专，浅则散。去国越境而师者，绝地也；四达者，衢地也；入深者，重地也；入浅者，轻地也；背固前隘者，围地也；无所往者，死地也。

是故散地，吾将一其志；轻地，吾将

使之属；争地，吾将趋其后；交地，
吾将谨其守；衢地，吾将固其结；重
地，吾将继其食；圯地，吾将进其涂；
围地，"吾将塞其阙；死地，吾将示
之以不活。

故兵之情，围则御，不得已则斗，过
则从。是故不知诸侯之谋者，不能预
交；不知山林、险阻、沮泽之形者，
不能行军；不用乡导者，不能得地利。
四五者，不知一，非霸王之兵也。夫
霸王之兵，伐大国，则其众不得聚；
威加于敌，则其交不得合。是故不争
天下之交，不养天下之权，信己之私，
威加于敌，故其城可拔，其国可隳。
施无法之赏，悬无政之令，犯三军之
众，若使一人。犯之以事，勿告以言；
犯之以利，勿告以害。

投之亡地然后存，陷之死地然后生。
夫众陷于害，然后能为胜败。

故为兵之事，在于顺详敌之意，并敌
一向，千里杀将，此谓巧能成事者也。

是故政举之日，夷关折符，无通其使；
厉于廊庙之上，以诛其事。敌人开阖，

必亟入之。先其所爱，微与之期。践
墨随敌，以决战事。是故始如处女，
敌人开户，后如脱兔，敌不及拒。

12、火攻篇 The Attack by Fire

XII. The Attack by Fire
火攻篇

Sun Tzu said: There are five ways of attacking with fire. The first objective is to burn enemy soldiers in their camp; the second objective is to burn supplies; the third objective is to burn a baggage vehicle; the fourth objective is to destroy arsenals; and the fifth objective is to dump fire on the enemy. To launch an attack, we must have the necessary resources. Fire-starting materials should always be readily available. There is an appropriate time for launching fire-based assaults and specific days for igniting a fire. The correct season is when the weather is extremely dry; the particular days are when the moon is in the constellations of the Ji, the Bi, the Yi, or the Zhen[19], since these are all days of

---

[19] The Ji, the Bi, the Yi, or the Zhen. They are different

increasing wind.

When assaulting with fire, one must be prepared for five potential outcomes: (1) When fire breaks out within the opposing camp, immediately launch an attack from the outside. (2) If there is an outbreak of fire, but the enemy soldiers keep silent, you should wait and refrain from attacking. (3) When the intensity of the flames reaches its peak, follow up with an attack if possible; otherwise, remain in place. (4) If it is feasible to attack with fire from the outside, do not wait for it to burst out from the inside; instead, strike at a suitable time. (5) When you build a fire, you should be in the upstream of the wind. Avoid attacking from the leeward. A daylight

____

names given to the moon in different positions by ancient Chinese astrological researchers. The moon's position in a certain position often had some kind of inspirational effect on the legitimacy of the regime, agricultural production, and divination.

wind is persistent, whereas a nighttime breeze is short-lived. Every army must be aware of the five developments related to fire, calculate the motions of the stars, and keep track of the dates.

Those who utilize fire as an assault aid demonstrate intellect, but those who use water as an attack aid develop strength. An opponent may be intercepted by water, but his possessions will not be taken. Unhappiness befalls a person who attempts to win conflicts and succeed in attacks without nurturing an entrepreneurial spirit, since the outcome is time-wasting and overall stagnation. Thus, the proverb: "The wise ruler makes long-range plans; the good general cultivates his resources." Do not move unless you sense an advantage; do not utilize your men unless there is something to gain; and do not fight unless the situation is dire. No monarch should send men into combat solely to indulge his own wrath, and no general should wage war out of spite. If it is advantageous to move forward, do so; otherwise, remain where you are. Anger can eventually be replaced by joy; irritation can be replaced by contentment. However, a once-destroyed state can never be reborn, nor can the dead be resurrected. Therefore, a wise ruler is vigilant, and a good general is full of caution. This is how to keep a state at peace and a strong army.

The original Chinese text

火攻篇

孙子曰：凡火攻有五：一曰火人，二曰火积，三曰火辎，四曰火库，五曰火队。行火必有因，烟火必素具。发火有时，起火有日。时者，天之燥也；日者，月在箕、壁、翼、轸也。凡此四宿者，风起之日也。

凡火攻，必因五火之变而应之。火发于内，则早应之于外。火发兵静者，待而勿攻，极其火力，可从而从之，不可从而止。火可发于外，无待于内，以时发之。火发上风，无攻下风。昼风久，夜风止。凡军必知有五火之变，以数守之。

故以火佐攻者明，以水佐攻者强。水可以绝，不可以夺。夫战胜攻取，而不修其功者凶，命曰费留。故曰：明主虑之，良将修之。非利不动，非得不用，非危不战。主不可以怒而兴师，将不可以愠而致战；合于利而动，不合于利而止。怒可以复喜，愠可以复悦；亡国不可以复存，死者不可以复生。故明君慎之，良将警之，此安国全军之道也。

13、用间篇 The Use of Spies

XIII. The Use of Spies
用间篇

Sun Tzu said: Recruiting a hundred thousand soldiers and marching them enormous distances is costly to the populace and a drain on the state's resources. The daily expenses will total one thousand troy ounces of silver. There will be turmoil both domestically and internationally, and men will collapse exhausted on the roadways. The labor of as many as 700,000 households will be hindered. Years may be spent by opposing armies vying for a victory that is determined in a single day. Given this, it is the height of inhumanity to stay ignorant about the enemy's plight because one resents spending one hundred ounces of silver on honors and emoluments. A person who behaves in this manner is not a leader of men, a present aid to his ruler, or a master of triumph. Thus, it is foresight that enables the wise monarch and the skillful general to attack and conquer, as well as to accomplish feats beyond the capability of ordinary men. This foresight cannot be derived from spirits, nor can it be learned inductively via experience or deductively through computation. The only way to know the dispositions of the adversary is to know the other men.

There are five types of spies: (1) local spies, (2) inward spies, (3) converted spies, (4) doomed spies, and (5) surviving spies. When all five types of spies are at work, the hidden system cannot be discovered. The term for this is "divine manipulation." It is the most valuable of the sovereign's faculties. Having local spies requires utilizing the services of a district's residents. Having inward spies and using hostile authorities. Having converted spies, obtaining and utilizing enemy spies for our own goals. Having doomed spies, doing some things publicly for purposes of deceit, and enabling our spies to know about them and report them to the adversary. Lastly, surviving spies are those who provide news from the enemy's camp.

As a result, no one in the army is required to cultivate more close relationships than spies. None should be more well compensated. In no other sector should more confidentiality be maintained. Spycraft is ineffective without a degree of intuitive sagacity. They cannot be controlled effectively without charity and candor. Without considerable mental inventiveness, one cannot be assured that their reports are accurate. Be subtle, and employ your spies for every type of operation. If a spy divulges confidential information before its proper time, both he and the person to whom he revealed the secret must be executed.

Whether the objective is to crush an army, storm a stronghold, or kill an individual, it is always important to begin by learning the names of the general in command's attendants, door-keepers, and sentries. These matters must be assigned to our spies.

The spies of the enemy who have come to spy on us must be tracked down, bribed, led away, and kept in comfort. Thus, they will turn into spies and become accessible for our service. Through the information provided by the converted spy, we are able to recruit and deploy local and foreign spies. Due to his intelligence, we are able to provide fake information to the enemy via the doomed spy. Lastly, the surviving spy's knowledge can be utilized on specific times. The purpose and goal of all five types of spy is knowledge of the opponent, and this knowledge can only be obtained first through a converted spy. Therefore, the converted spy must be handled with the utmost tolerance.

Historically, the emergence of the Yin[20] dynasty was owing to Yi Zhi[21]'s service under the Xia[22]. Similarly, the emergence of the Zhou dynasty was a result of Lv Ya[23]'s service under the Yin. Therefore, only an intelligent ruler and a shrewd general will employ the greatest level of

---

[20] The Yin Dynasty (about 1300 B.C. - about 1046 B.C.) is an ancient Chinese dynasty, also known as Shang. It is later replaced by Zhou dynasty.
[21] Yi Zhi (? - 1550 B.C.), also known as Yi Yin. An ancient Chinese statesman and contributor to the founding of the Yin Dynasty.
[22] The Xia Dynasty (about 2070 B.C. - about 1600 B.C.) is the first hereditary dynasty recorded in Chinese history. It is later replaced by the Yin dynasty.
[23] Lv Ya (? - 1015 B.C.), also known as Jiang Ziya. Ancient Chinese statesman and contributor to the founding of the Zhou Dynasty.

military intelligence for spy, achieving enormous benefits. The mobility of an army is contingent upon spies.

The original Chinese text

用间篇

孙子曰：凡兴师十万，出征千里，百姓之费，公家之奉，日费千金；内外骚动，怠于道路，不得操事者，七十万家。相守数年，以争一日之胜，而爱爵禄百金，不知敌之情者，不仁之至也，非人之将也，非主之佐也，非胜之主也。故明君贤将，所以动而胜人，成功出于众者，先知也。先知者，不可取于鬼神，不可象于事，不可验于度，必取于人，知敌之情者也。

故用间有五：有因间，有内间，有反间，有死间，有生间。五间俱起，莫知其道，是谓神纪，人君之宝也。因间者，因其乡人而用之。内间者，因其官人而用之。反间者，因其敌间而用之。死间者，为诳事于外，令吾间

知之，而传于敌间也。生间者，反报
也。

故三军之事，莫亲于间，赏莫厚于间，
事莫密于间。非圣智不能用间，非仁
义不能使间，非微妙不能得间之实。
微哉！微哉！无所不用间也。间事未
发，而先闻者，间与所告者皆死。

凡军之所欲击，城之所欲攻，人之所
欲杀，必先知其守将，左右，谒者，
门者，舍人之姓名，令吾间必索知之。

必索敌人之间来间我者，因而利之，
导而舍之，故反间可得而用也。因是
而知之，故乡间、内间可得而使也；
因是而知之，故死间为诳事，可使告
敌。因是而知之，故生间可使如期。
五间之事，主必知之，知之必在于反
间，故反间不可不厚也。

昔殷之兴也，伊挚在夏；周之兴也，
吕牙在殷。故惟明君贤将，能以上智
为间者，必成大功。此兵之要，三军
之所恃而动也。